Pep Guardiola's Positional Grid

Team Training Exercises using the Positional Grid

By Marcus DiBernardo

Table of Contents

Explanation of Guardiola's Positional Soccer

Positional soccer provides a set of guidelines and structure for the attacking phase of the game. The positional soccer field is divided into vertical and horizontal zones that indicate positional responsibilities for the players. The interesting thing about positional soccer is that the player's options to some extent are predetermined by the position of the ball. The central theme behind positional soccer is to create superiority of numbers in a specific area of the field, using mainly shorter range passing. If a team can fully shift the opponent by drawing them to one side of the field with short passing, the opportunity to attack the weak side becomes the objective. Guardiola spoke about this aspect of positional play saying, "the objective is to move the opponent, not the ball. The secret is to overload one side of the pitch so the opponent must tilt its own defense to cope. When you've done that, we attack and score from the other side. That's why you have to pass the ball with a clear intention. Draw in the opponent, then hit them with the sucker punch." The tactics Guardiola speaks about sound simple but in order to accomplish this way of playing, the team structure must be correct. Guardiola believed in order to build the proper team structure, the team would need to complete roughly 15 passes, this would fully create an attacking team shape. In tactical periodization this would be called the attacking organization phase. Once the teams positioning in attack was established, if they lost the ball, the players are already in a good position to press the ball to win it back. This is one of the important aspects of positional soccer that makes it so effective. The former Barcelona great, Johan Cruyff was asked, how do Barcelona win the ball back so quickly? He replied, "It's because they don't have to run back more than 10 meters as they never pass the ball more than 10 meters." That statement alone sheds some light into the secret of positional soccer, with and without the ball. The secret in possession is positioning and the secret on defense is positioning.

Positional play is an important aspect that has influenced Guardiola's tactics over the years, but to fully appreciate Guardiola, you must grasp an understanding of the ideas behind positional soccer, tiki-taka soccer, total football and the Barcelona way. In fact, when Guardiola was leaving Barcelona as the manager, he credited his work to, "being built on the shoulders of giants." What Guardiola meant was that he didn't create the way Barcelona played, he only put his influence on what was already built, because long before Guardiola, the likes of Johan Cruyff and Rinus Michels helped forge the style of Barcelona. Johan Cruyff is most commonly credited with creating the Barcelona style of play, but it was Rinus Michels that influenced Cruyff's soccer ideas. Michels coached Cruyff at Barcelona from 1971-1975, and also in 1974 for the famous Dutch national team that introduced "Total Football" to the world. Michels stressed the importance of interchanging positions, attacking with the pass and the dribble, and relentless defensive pressing. When Cruyff became the Head Coach of Barcelona in 1988, he built on the ideas of Rinus Michels, developing the Barcelona philosophy even further. The style Cruyff developed became known as tiki-taka soccer, and it brought Barcelona instant success. The tiki-taka style was later adopted and used by the Spain national teams, under Del Bosque and Aragones. After Cruyff, it was Louis Van Gaal and Frank Rijkaard who further developed the Barcelona philosophy of play. Rijkaard made adjustments to the tiki-taka system, mixing it with positional soccer, as Barcelona continued to be one of the world's best teams. After Rijkaard left Barcelona, in came the new manager Pep Guardiola. Guardiola revolutionized Barcelona in 2008, as they won almost everything between 2008-2012. Pep brought his own version of tiki taka, positional play and extreme pressing to Barcelona. However, Guardiola had something nobody before him had at Barcelona, Lionel Messi. Messi brought another dimension to Guardiola's tactics, a dimension that made Barcelona almost unstoppable. Opposing coaches could pick the perfect defensive game plan, but in the end, no game plane could contain Messi. Pep would go on to win everything at Barcelona and later move onto to Germany and then England.

When Guardiola moved to Manchester City in the EPL, he was forced to reinvent his tactics. The English Premier League is not Spain or Germany, it demands speed and power, along with the ability to play in many types of challenging environments. At Manchester City Guardiola selected players with exceptional speed to play across the backline, especially at wingback, his wingers were also very fast, along with pace at the striker position. Guardiola chose a defensive center midfielder with mobility, toughness and speed, while the other two center midfielders were his most technical players in the team. The amazing thing about this Manchester City team was how they were able to play Pep's new version of positional soccer, made specifically for the EPL. You could see the individual players getting better every week in the system, as the team started to play exciting and entertaining soccer. However, this Manchester City team was more vertical then his teams at Barcelona, they looked to get in and behind the opponents more than any Barcelona team had. The other incredible factor is that at Barcelona most of the players had been groomed in the system of play their entire careers, while at Manchester City

Pep taught the team from scratch. In my opinion, Manchester City might have showcased Pep's greatest work as a coach. It proved that positional soccer could be taught and perfected in a short time frame at the highest level.

What is the Guardiola Positional Grid?

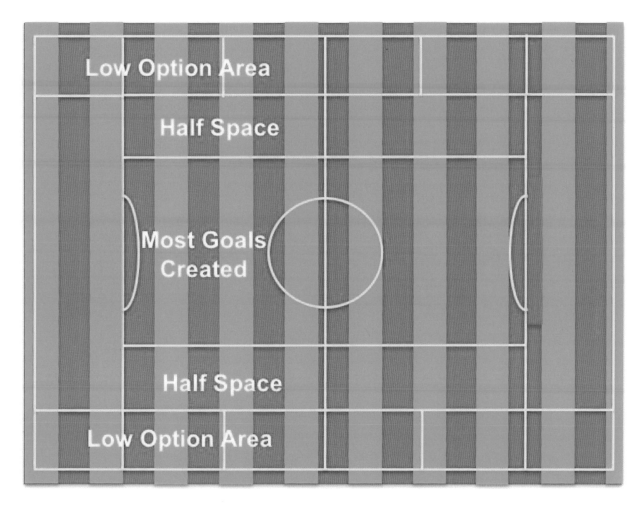

The positional grid is like a cognitive road map for players when in possession. Depending on where the ball is located, players are responsible to fill a specific a location in the positional grid. The end result is that a team shape or structure will develop in possession, resulting in a positional soccer style of play. However, the game of soccer has unlimited ever changing situations and variables, so there will always be freedom within the provided positional structure to make adaptions. The positional soccer grid divides the training pitch into 20 sections, basically five vertical rows and four cross-field sections. The widest channels are referred to as the low option areas, because there are limited passing opportunities that can made from out wide. The widest areas are utilized often to draw the defense out, moving them from side to side to open up spaced in between the defenders or on the far side. The next space that borders the wide channel is called a "half space". The half space is a dangerous area because penetrating balls and shots on goal can be taken from this position. Guardiola often liked his most dangerous players like Robben or Messi to receive the ball in the half spaces. How many goals have we seen those two players create by cutting inside and shooting to the far post! The next space is the large space on top of the 18-yard box, this space is considered the most dangerous area on the soccer field. This large box is so dangerous because more goals are created from this area than anywhere else. However, quick 1-touch play is critical in this area to be effective, with the largest concentration of defenders located in this space. Of course players like Messi are invaluable in areas like this, as they can make the impossible happen, changing the game.

The positional grid offers a structure and provides cues for players, letting them know to adjust their position depending in which zone the ball is in, they must know when to fill an empty zone when it has been vacated, or to move into a zone to create superiority of numbers. A general rule of thumb is that no more than three players will be in a horizontal line, and not more than two in a vertical line, this helps give the player on the ball two-three passing options. The entire game can be taught using the grid, from build-up play to the attacking third. When using the grid to teach positional soccer there are many ways to utilize it. One way is to set-up trainings that require players to operate inside the positional grid, adhering to specific conditions, but still allowing a degree tactical freedom while encouraging problem solving. An example of this would be requiring five shorter passes on one side of the field before a long pass can be made, switching the field to the far wide player. The next type of training can use the grid as more of

specific road map that must be strictly adhered to. An example of this would be working on

playing the ball out of the back. Each player will be assigned a specific part of the grid to be in,

as a standard way of operating out of the back is established. The other beneficial aspect of

using the positional grid is that it organizes space on the field in a realistic way for players.

When players train tactics in specific game realistic spaces, their soccer awareness, tactical

sense and soccer IQ benefit. Training in the positional grid helps players better judge distance,

space and time in relationship to carrying out the desired tactics. I recommend training with the

grid and then removing the grid at the end, so that spatial relationship is further reinforced.

Important: The exercises in this book can be modified to create different outcomes and player

experiences. Also, Guardiola most often used a 4-3-3 formation, so this book is written

demonstrating a 4-3-3, but you can choose to teach any formation in the positional grid. The

grid can also be modified to teach younger players who play 7v7 or 9v9.

I hope you enjoy the book and be creative in the ways you use the positional grid. Feel free to

reach out to me with any questions at coachdibernardo@gmail.com

Exercise #1
Switching the Field to Wide Winger

Field: ½ field with CB's able to drop 10 yards deeper
Players: 10v7 + Keeper

For this exercise a center line (white dotted line) is added to the positional grid. The black team in possession must complete a minimum of five passes before looking to switch the field to the far side winger. By drawing the defensive team in using short passing, the black team is effectively setting up to attack on the opposite side of the field. Institute the rule in this exercise that the far side winger must stay in the widest outside channel. When the long ball is played across the field to the far winger, another player must fill the channel next to the winger in support. This support player is very important in positional soccer, because the support player has better forward vision and an easier ability to play forward penetrating passes. The support player also provides an immediate pass back option for the winger, which gives an outlet away from defensive pressure. There are many attacking options available once the ball is switched to the far side winger, which I will go over in the following diagrams. But for this exercise, the attacking team must connect a minimum of five short passes before switching the ball to the far side winger. Make the rule that when the ball is switched to the far side winger after five passes, there must be a player in close support filling the half space in the next channel. If the attack is not on, the team will look to connect a minimum of five more passes before switching the ball to the opposite side winger, as play continues. If the defense wins the ball they can score on either small sided goal located at half field. The black team in possession is allowed to drop their CB's back behind the half field line, the defending team is not allowed to cross half field, this will allow the black team in possession to properly build-up play. Feel vary the exercise by adding or subtracting defenders

In the below diagram the center midfielder, located in the half space, is in direct support of the right winger with the ball. Notice the left winger on the far side has stayed wide, in a good position to attack the defense when they have shifted. The left winger will most likely be supported by the left wingback when the long pass is played cross field to the winger. This type of play is fundamental in positional soccer.

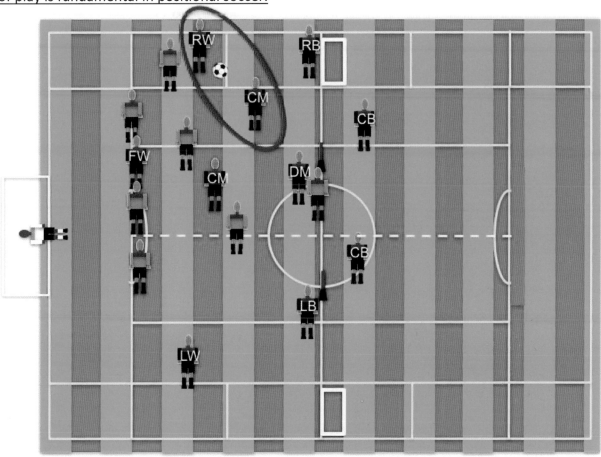

Here we see the left winger supported by the center midfielder in the half space, as the left back is directly behind in vertical support. This demonstrates the positional soccer idea of two players in a vertical channel and only three horizontally across. Notice the defensive center mid (pink circle) is in a good position to hit a pass to the far right side winger, after the defense is drawn in by the short passing.

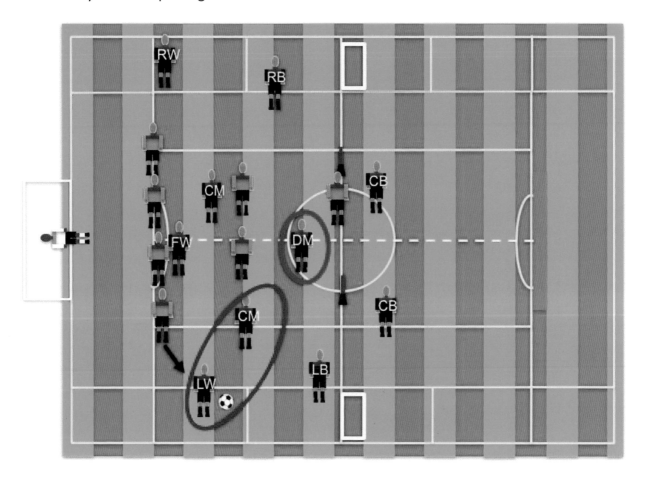

Now that we established the positional soccer objectives of this exercise, short passing to draw the defense to one side, then attacking wide on the far side. We will now look at some possible movement ideas from the long pass that switches the field. This diagram shows the defensive center midfielder passing the ball wide to the winger, who plays a quick pass to the center midfielder who is in support in the half space area. The winger sprints by the committed defender and receives the pass back from the supporting center midfielder. This movement leads to an organized and well planned attack in the box. The winger attacks by driving the end line, as attacking players will cover the near post, far post and area diagonally back between the penalty spot and the top of 18-yard box. Anytime a player drives the end-line, these three areas are always covered in Guardiola's attacking tactics.

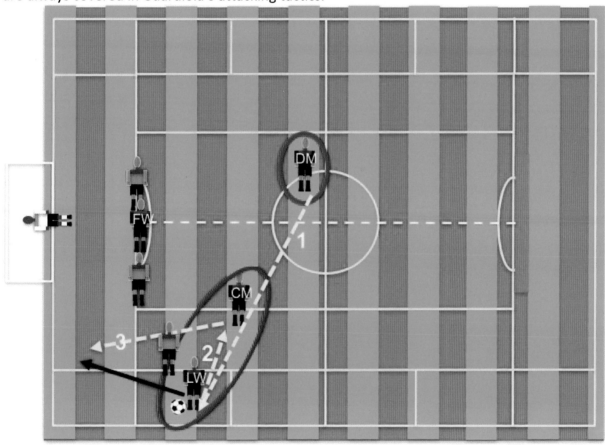

In this example the center midfielder leaves his supporting position in the half space to exploit the space behind the pressuring defender. The winger recognizes the center midfielders run and delivers a penetrating pass to the center midfielder.

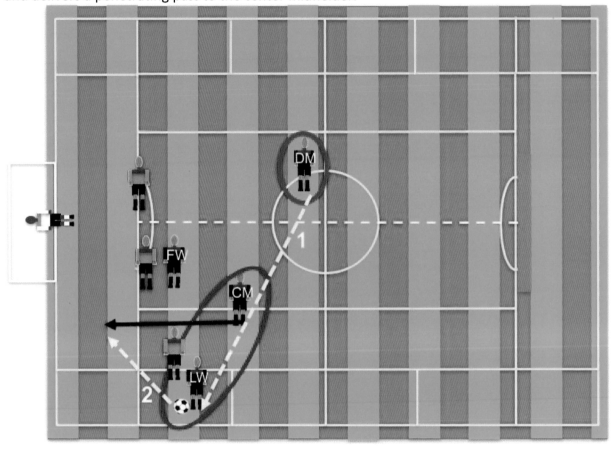

Here is another common theme in positional soccer. The winger receives the long pass from the defensive center midfielder, who switches the field; in this case the winger does not receive immediate pressure from the defender, so the winger runs towards the box with the ball. When a defender comes to give pressure, the winger plays a wall pass off a player in the central area, and continues to penetrate the box receiving the ball back. As the winger penetrates the box, his teammates make sure the far post, near post and area diagonally backwards is covered.

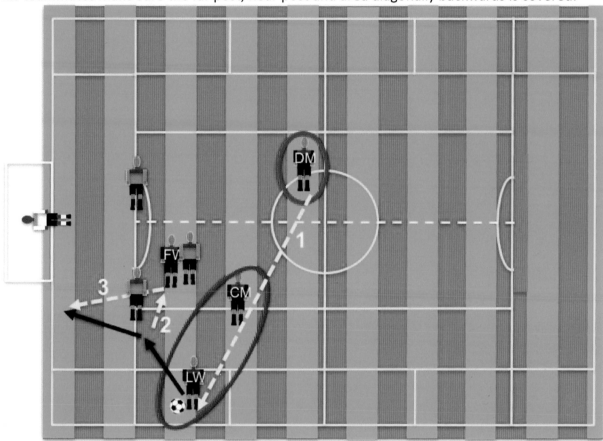

This example includes the winger, center midfielder and left wingback. The ball is played long into the winger, who controls it and starts to take the defender inside with his touch. Instead of using his inside support player, the winger plays a ball down the channel to the overlapping wingback. All the rules of positional soccer are recognized in this example, as the winger is wide with inside support and no more than two players are in the same vertical channel.

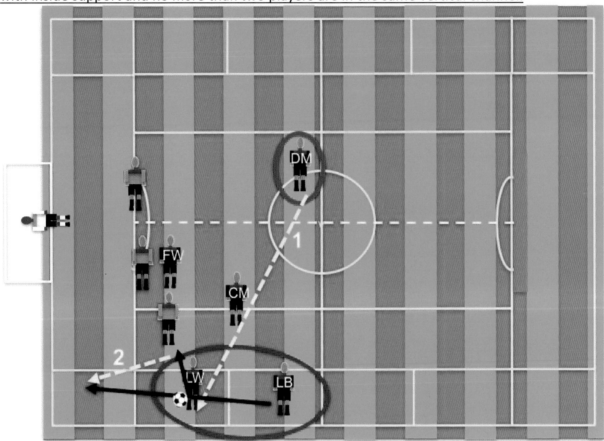

Exercise #2
Creating Overloads in Central Attacking Area

Field: ½ field
Players: 10v7 + Keeper

This exercise requires that a minimum of two players be in the central attacking zone at all times. <u>The central zone is from the top of the 18-yard box to the white dotted line, and must be filled by two-three players at all times in the attack</u>. This rule will encourage combination play in the central part of the box, the interchanging of players in and out of the box, and helps exploit the space in between the defending lines. Notice there is a 3v2 attacking overload in both parts of the central zone. <u>Require all five vertical zones be filled in possession.</u> <u>If the ball is played wide, make sure a center midfielder slides into the half space to support the wide winger</u>, as the wingback supports from behind, <u>making two players in the vertical in the wide channel</u>. If the defending team wins the ball, they can attempt to score on either of the two small goals at half field.

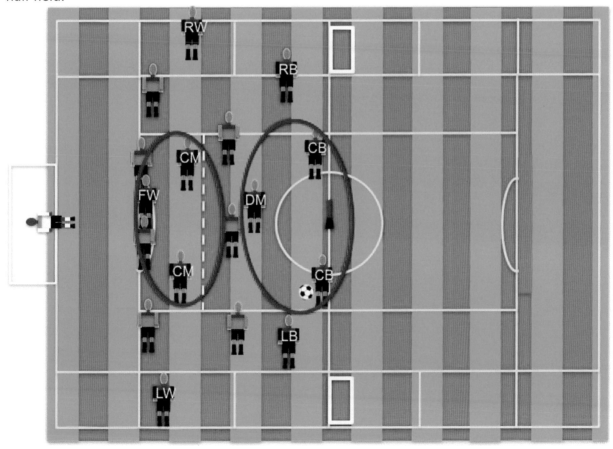

Exercise #3
Ensuring Attacking Width by Filling Half Spaces

Field: ½ field
Players: 10v7 + Keeper

This exercise does not require a certain number of passes on one side to switch the field or to overload the central attacking zone, this exercise gives a little more freedom from the previous exercise but still utilizes the fundamentals of positional soccer. The black team in possession must have all five vertical lanes filled, no more than two players in the same outside vertical lane and no more than three players in line across the field, at least one player must be staggered out of the line if more than three players are involved. Using these rules will ensure proper spacing, good width in attack and proper team structure in attack. Encourage player rotation in possession, so players will be trained to fill spaces that are left empty. If the defense wins the ball they will look to score on either of the small-sided goals located at half field. Feel free to add variations to any of the exercises. Examples: 1-touch only in central zone, 1-touch from winger to support player in half space, if wingers take 2-touches they must cut inside as another player overlaps the outside channel.

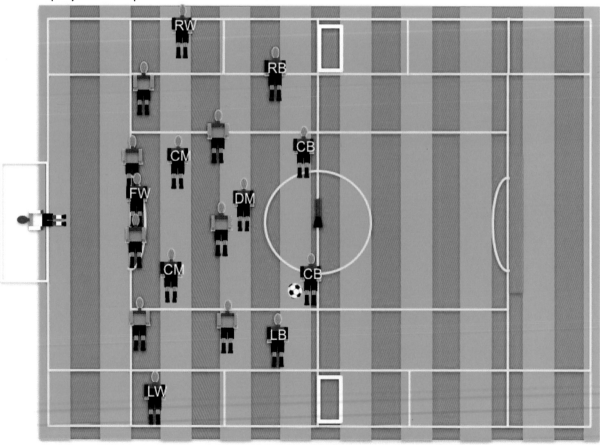

Exercise #4
Creating Attacking Team Structure in 15 Passes

Field: 3/4 field
Players: 10v7 + Keeper

Guardiola often said it takes a minimum of 15 passes to create the attacking structure needed in positional soccer. In this exercise the team in black must complete 15 passes before they can shoot on goal. After 15 consecutive passes, the entire team must be in the opponent's half of the field, set up in their attacking shape. Require all four of the outside vertical wide areas be occupied during the build-up. The idea is to pass the ball, pushing the defense backwards, as the attacking structure takes shape. Once the team structure is set up in the attacking 1/3, the team can look to penetrate from switching the ball out wide, creating overloads that can exploited or by attacking spaces that appear in the defense. When the orange defensive team regains possession, they will try and score on any of the four counter goals or by completing six consecutive passes. The black team must press the ball, trying to win it back immediately after losing possession. The black teams center backs are allowed to drop deeper than the red marker, the orange team is not allowed to press higher than the red marker. A variation would be to add a keeper below the red marker to help build the attack. Another variation is after the team has advanced into the attacking half, having made 15 passes with the attacking structure established, institute the rule of a minimum of five passes on one side of the field before looking to switch the ball to the far side, as the half space must be filled in support of the winger.

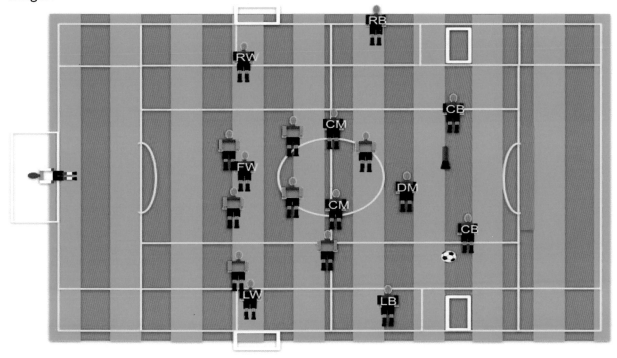

Exercise #5
1-touch Combination Play in the Central Attacking Zone

Field: ½ field with CB's able to drop 10 yards deeper
Players: 10v8 + Keeper

This exercise trains quick play in the central attacking zone of the field. This zone is often referred to as zone 14, it is the area where most assists come from. Data shows that the majority of assists come through this central attacking zone in 2.7 seconds or less. If the ball is kept in the middle zone for longer than 8 seconds, the chance of creating a goal is very small. If a penetrating ball or shot can't be taken from the central zone quickly, the ball should be passed out wide. In this exercise, a white dotted line is added to the positional grid to highlight zone 14. To start the exercise do not allow the two center midfielders on defense to drop below that dotted line in the central zone, and only the center backs on orange can be in the central zone, the outside defensive backs are not allowed to squeeze into the central zone, this will create room to be exploited by the black team's center midfielders. To increase the difficulty, of the exercise, allow one orange center midfielder to drop below the white line into the central zone. The black center midfielders are free to rotate to exploit the spaces in between the defensive lines. This is another exercise where all <u>five vertical zones need to be filled in attack</u>. In this example, notice the 3v2 overload in the top half of the central zone above the white line. <u>One variation you can try is to make the central zone area below the dotted line a 1-touch box.</u> When the defense wins the ball they score by completing six passes or playing into a counter goal.

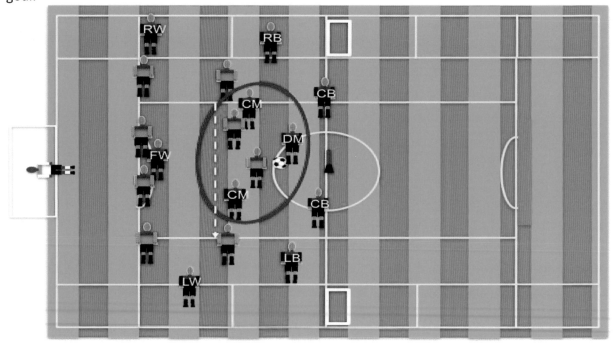

Below are two examples of quick 1-touch play in the central attacking zone. Example One) a penetrating pass is hit by the defensive center midfielder, as the left center midfielder runs forward to combine with the striker in quick combination play, then another quick penetrating pass is played to the left winger cutting in

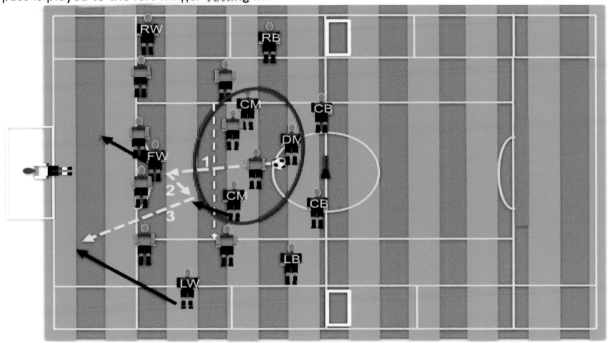

Example Two) The defensive center midfielder plays a penetrating ball into the striker as both center midfielders go forward in support of the striker. Notice the combination play that ends up with the striker getting in and behind the defense. This play is quick and well under the 8 seconds the statistics show to be effective.

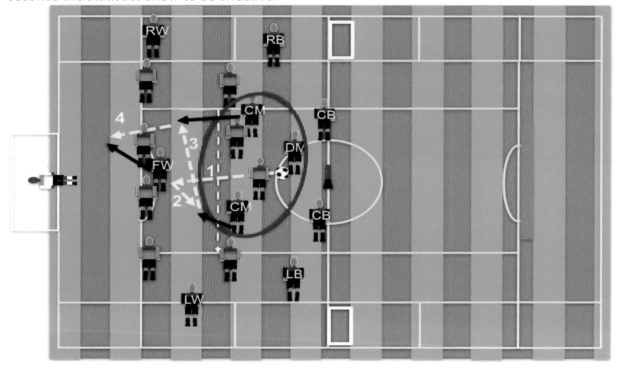

Here is the same exercise but the numbers have been reduced to 8v7 + Keeper.

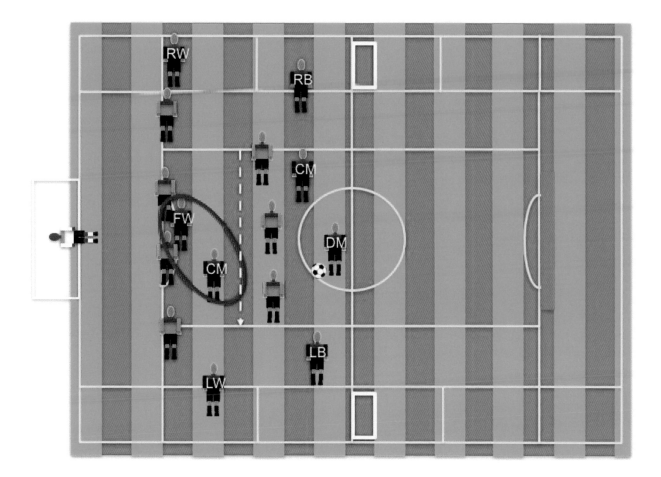

Exercise #6
Working the Ball Out from the Back using the Positional Grid

Field: Entire Field
Players: 11 v 11

This exercise uses the positional grid to teach starting points for players when working the ball out of the back from a goal kick. The starting points can be changed based upon personnel, formation, defensive numbers and the general ideas of the coach. These are the starting positions for players that Guardiola often uses at Manchester City in a 4-3-3 formation. Notice all five vertical channels are filled. The goalkeeper is critical to the success of working the ball out from the back, because the keeper is the player that creates numerical superiority against the pressing defenders. Both center backs split the sides of the box, the defensive center mid adopts a side-on position on top of the box, the two of the center midfielders occupy both half space areas on top of the box, the wingbacks create the largest width in the back, as the wingers and striker start in off-sides positions, behind the opponents back three or four. By having the wingers and striker starting behind the defensive back line, it makes it very difficult on the back line defenders, because the defenders won't be able see the ball and the person they are marking at the same time. This will result in the defenders having to constantly swivel their head around to keep track of the attackers. This goal kick starting position is very dangerous to the defense for a number of reasons. If the initial seven defenders are beaten, it becomes a fast 3v3 attack with lots of space available behind the back three to exploit. Notice that with this starting position on goal kicks, the middle of the field is wide open, the keeper can elect to deliver a long ball to the front three, bypassing the seven pressuring defenders. Guardiola's Manchester City team is built for taking advantage of these quick attacks, because their front three players are so fast. The new Manchester City keeper was specially selected for his excellent passing ability, both long and short range. This adds yet another dimension to the City attack, forcing the defense to respect the keepers short and long accurate passing ability. Notice that positional soccer can be played from the goal kick, but so can a very vertical and direct attack. This is one of the ways that Guardiola has adapted his tactics over time.

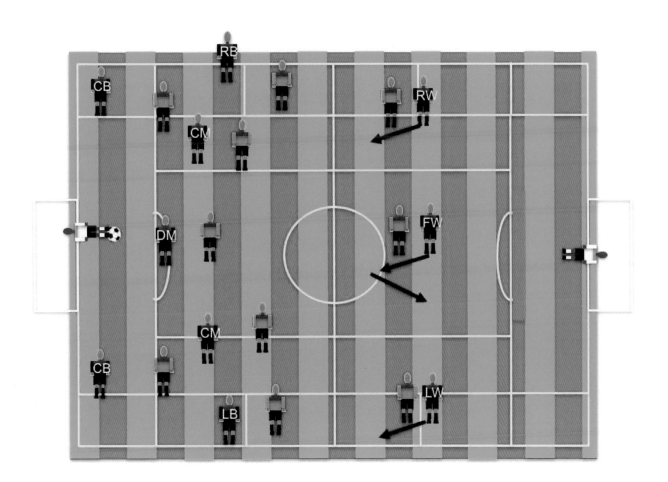

Exercise #7
7v5 Positional Grid Working the Ball Out of the Back

Working the Ball Out from the Back: 7v5+Keepers. The black team always starts play with a goal kick. The orange team uses a 3:1:2 formation attempting to high press the black team from the goal kick. The game is played like a regular game, but all restarts and throw-ins begin with a goal kick for the black team.

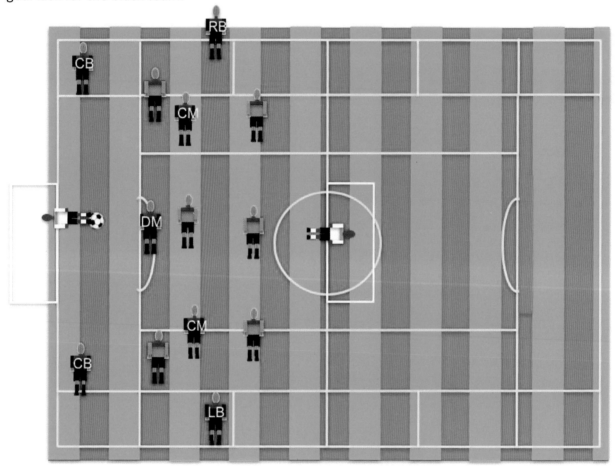

Exercise #8
Pattern Play using the Positional Grid to Stimulate Movement Ideas

Pattern play is an excellent way to stimulate team attacking movement ideas that fit a system of play. The below example shows a pattern that teaches many of the principles of positional soccer. The pattern has players filling all five vertical channels, uses short quick passing to attract the defense followed by a longer pass to switch the field to the wide winger, as a center midfielder offers support in the half space, the winger plays the support player and receives a pass down the channel. The movement ends with the winger crossing the ball into three players who cover the three zones in the box. When training pattern play, work the same pattern, but on the opposite side every other possession.

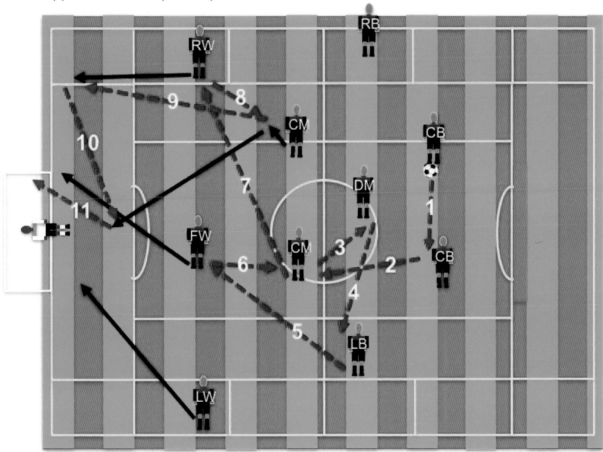

Pattern Play Variation: In this pattern the winger attacks the box off the dribble, plays a combination towards the center of the box, and continues to drive the end-line. The wingback will overlap, as the opposite side winger crashes the far post, and the striker and center midfielders crash the box. This pattern emphasizes many positional play concepts: the far side winger crashing the back post, diagonal backwards support provided in the box for finishing, the overlapping player down the channel and the quick combination play of the winger off the dribble.

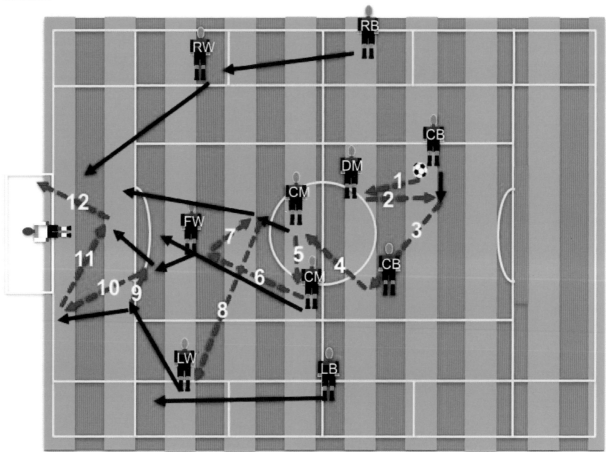

Exercise #9
Pattern Play using Smaller Numbers

This simple pattern uses six attacking players. Notice the quick 1-touch combination play in the central area followed by a pass played wide to the winger, who drives the box and whips in a ball to the far post.

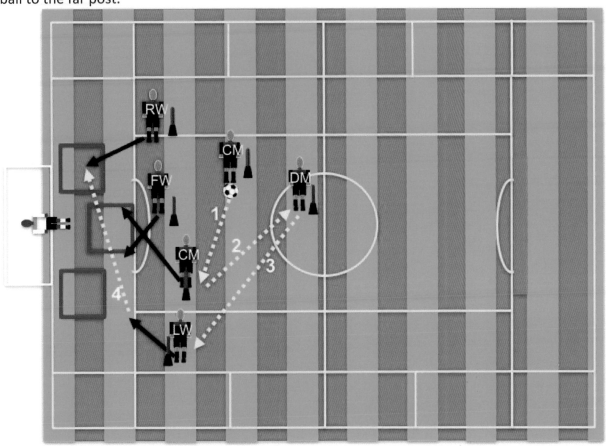

Variation: You can rotate every other repetition using this variation. The center midfielder plays into the center midfielder, who 1-touches to the defensive center midfielder, the defensive center midfielder plays wide to the winger, the winger dribbles inside, playing a 1-2 combination off the center midfielder, and then crosses into one of the three scoring zones.

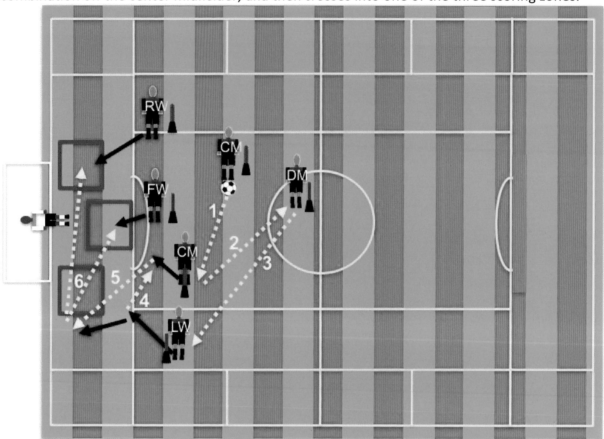

Exercise #10
Color Coded Positional Shadow Play

Notice that each area of the grid is coded a different color. I create this on the field by using different color disc cones. Starting from the keeper the coach yells out the section color that the pass is to played into. Once play is started, the coach directs the entire sequence by shouting out the section color that the ball must be played into next. Players will adjust their positioning in possession according to the location of the ball. There are many variations that can be added to color coded shadow play, including touch restrictions, 1-touch squares identified, long ball required, short ball required, 15 passes before scoring, 1-touch scoring or scoring only from a cross.

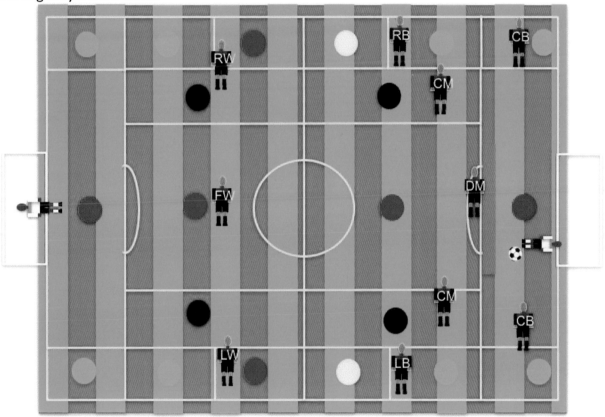

Variation of color coded shadow play: The coach directs the shadow play in one half only, when the ball crosses into the opponent's half, the shadow play is freely carried out by the players with no direction from the coach.

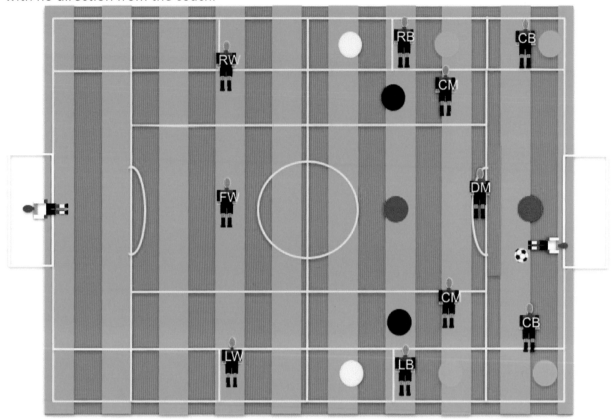

11v6 Shadow Play: Opposed shadow play can be strictly passive or it can become more aggressive, it depends on what the coach wants. The addition of six defenders makes shadow play more challenging and realistic. The defense is not allowed to win the ball, rather they are there to cut off passing angles and provide an off-sides line.

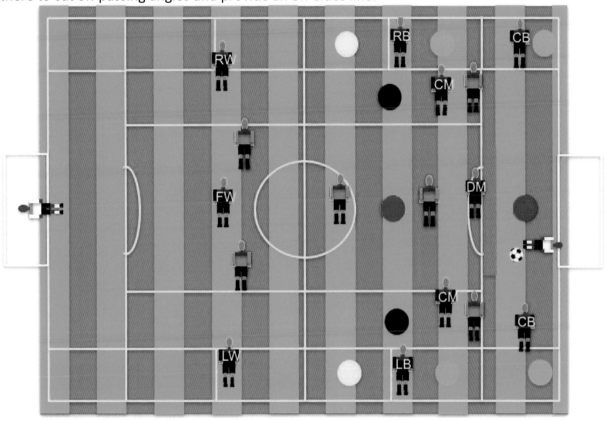

Exercise #11
Positional Grid Finishing

This is a standard finishing exercise used by Guardiola at Barcelona. In this exercise the right side performs the first movement, using the right back, right winger, two center midfielders (one located up top playing as a striker) and a striker. The right back plays a ball to feet to the center midfielder who is checking in between the lines. The center midfielder lays the ball off 1-touch to the supporting center midfielder, this cues the right winger to pull backwards off the red marker (red markers symbolize defenders), the center midfielder plays a pass to the wingers back foot, as the winger drives the end lIne, crossing the ball into one of the three designated finishing areas. This exercise teaches that when the ball is dribbled to the end line, players making runs into the box must cover the near post, the area diagonally backwards towards the penalty spot and the far post. Covering all three of these areas are an important part of positional soccer. After the right side performs the movement, the left side will go next. This exercise can be done with up to twelve players rotating. Two sets of players can take turns up top, and two sets of wing backs can be used, both pairs sharing repetitions.

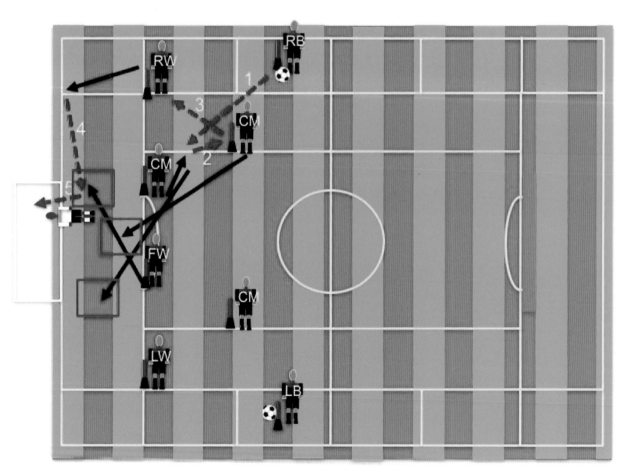

Progression: The winger now cuts inside, as the wingback overlaps down the channel to receive the pass from the center midfielder. The wingback dribbles the end line, delivering a ball into one of the three finishing areas.

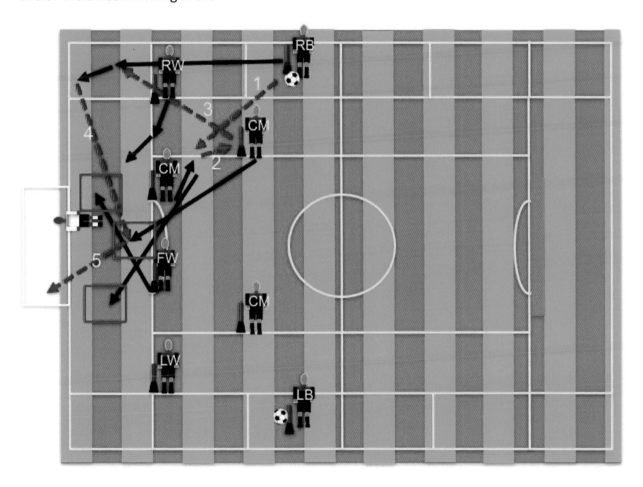

Printed in Great Britain
by Amazon